Saint Nikolai Velimirović

I0108356

Saint Nikolai Velimirović "The New Chrysostom"

HIS LIFE AND SERVICE

The Life by Fr. Daniel M. Rogich

The Service by Mother Macaria
a Nun of the Serbian Orthodox Church

ST. XENIA MONASTIC COMMUNITY
INDIANAPOLIS, INDIANA
2018

Printed with the blessing of His Grace
✠ Longin
Serbian Orthodox Bishop of the Diocese
of New Gracanica and Midwestern America

Copyright © 2018 by St. Xenia Monastic Community

The Life: copyright © 1993 by the St. Herman of Alaska Brotherhood
Reproduced, with minor editorial changes, by their kind permission.

All rights reserved.
Printed in the United States of America.
For information about permission to reproduce selections from this book, write to the street or e-mail address below:

St. Xenia Monastic Community
1901 N. Pennsylvania St.
Indianapolis, IN 46202-1417

mk@westoncounseling.org

Front cover: The mosaic from the marker of St. Nikolai's original grave on the south side of St. Sava Monastery Church in Libertyville, Illinois. Photo courtesy of Fr. Alexii (Altschul).
Back cover: St. Sava Monastery Church. After the Serbian Orthodox Diocese of America was established, Bp. Nikolai Velimirović encouraged Bp. Mardarije, the first bishop of the new diocese, to purchase land north of Chicago. This is where St. Sava's was built, housing also a seminary and printing press. Later in his life, Bp. Nikolai taught at the seminary.
Orthodox Ornaments: By permission of *The Orthodox Arts Journal.*

St. Xenia Monastic Community
ISBN-13: 978-0-9983906-4-2

BISAC: REL052010
Religion / Prayerbooks / Christian

CONTENTS

PREFACE

St. Nikolai Velimirović was hailed by many of his contemporaries as "the New Chrysostom." He both was a scion of Serbia and remains a burning light of the Universal Church. St. Nikolai was also a "Renaissance Man" in the best sense of the term, without letting his scholarly achievement undermine his full-hearted commitment to our Lord Jesus Christ.

In addition to his native Serbian, St. Nikolai was fluent in six languages, including German, English, French, and Russian. Thus he was equipped to be an ambassador for Orthodoxy in the West, both in Europe and in the United States. His power of persuasion lay, not only in rhetoric, but in the sheer beauty of his divine words. He was a poet at heart and had a poetic insight into this world and the world to come. He had the power to lift people out of their mundane realities into his cosmic vision. Some of his most profound verse is born of deep suffering.

St. Nikolai, who lived from 1880–1956, did not escape the horrors of World War II. He was imprisoned in Dachau and released by American troops, only to find himself without a homeland. He found shelter in the U.S. for his last decade, during which time he lectured at four Ortho-dox seminaries: St. Sava's, Holy Trinity, St. Vladimir's, and St. Tikhon's. And he was the first instructor to do so in the English language, removing barriers for American-born seminarians and enriching the formation of a generation of Orthodox clergy.

The life by Fr. Daniel Rogich that follows is among the first to be published in English. It reached significant readership through *The Orthodox Word,* endearing St. Nikolai to many. That alone is sufficient reason to reproduce it here 25 years later. But more than that, the text was a fertile ground of inspiration for the liturgical service that follows. It provided many windows into the Saint's particular expression of sanctity.

In honor of St. Nikolai, the sisters of the St. Xenia Monastic Community are very happy to provide a service originally written in English, the language of the Saint's adopted home, a language in which he preached, wrote, taught, and missionized.

Allow me to share a deeply personal joy as well: St. Nikolai spoke at St. Philip's Episcopal Church in Harlem in the 1920s, some 30 years before my father was assigned pastor there. Since learning that I grew up in a parish where a Serbian Saint and people of

African descent shared a spiritual encounter, I have attributed my conversion to Holy Orthodoxy, and my finding a home in the Serbian Orthodox Archdiocese in particular, to the loving prayers which St. Nikolai offered long before my birth. Thus it is with deep feeling and gratitude that all of us sisters, each touched by the Saint in a personal way, have worked together to bring these texts into print, aided by the generous help of our clergy advisor, Fr. Marko Bojović.

We sincerely hope that the life and service of St. Nikolai Velimirović will be a vehicle for him to bless you also in a unique and personal way. Holy St. Nikolai pray to God for us!

—Nun Katherine, Superior

Serbian Pronunciation Hints

C c	"ts" as in tsar		Š š	"sh" as in sugar
Č č	"ch" as in chalk		Ž ž	"zh" as in azure & pleasure
Ć ć	"ch" as in church		*Diphthongs*	
H h	"kh," a guttural "h"		aj	"ay" as in cayak
J j	"y" as in yes		ej	"ey" as in grey
R r	as a vowel, "r" as in er		oj	"oy" as in boy

The Life of Our Holy Father
St. Nikolai Velimirović

"THE NEW CHRYSOSTOM"
BISHOP OF OHRID AND ŽIČA

Commemorated March 5/18 and April 20/May 3 (†1956)

By Fr. Daniel M. Rogich

Beloved, even if we should attain the very pinnacle of virtue, let us consider ourselves least of all, as we have learned that pride is able to cast down even from the heavens the person who does not take heed, and humility of mind is able to bring up on High from the very abyss of sin the person who knows how to be sober. For this is what placed the Publican before the Pharisee. By pride I mean an overwhelming boastful spirit, surpassing even incorporeal powers, that of the devil himself, while humility of mind and acknowledgment of sins by the robber is what brought him into Paradise before the Apostles.
—St. John Chrysostom

HERE, IN THE FIFTEENTH anniversary year of his glorification, we present the Life of a modern Serbian Saint who was a missionary to America, coming to this land four times, spending the last eleven years of his life here, and finally dying on American soil. Bishop Nikolai was canonized by the Serbian Orthodox Church in 2003.* He is remembered by American Orthodox Christians as a protector, mover and inspirer of the Serbian Orthodox Church in America, as an instructor at the St. Sava Seminary in Libertyville, Illinois, as the dean and rector of the St. Tikhon of Zadonsk Seminary in South Canaan, Pennsylvania, and as the author of the valuable *Prologue of Ohrid,* which has been published in English, first in four and, now, in two volumes.

---

* Since 1987 he had been celebrated as a Saint at the local level by his native diocese. [St. Xenia Editors.]

OUR HOLY and God-bearing father, Bishop Nikolai of blessed memory, was born at dawn on December 23, 1880, on the feast of St. Naum of Ohrid, to pious Serbian Orthodox parents, Dragomir and Katarina Velimirović, in the small village of Lelić, only five miles southwest of Valjevo, a city located in the valley of the Povlen Mountains of western Serbia. Because he was born physically weak, this divine child of God was baptized soon after his birth. He was given the name Nikola, after his family's "Krsna Slava" (family Patron Saint), "Sveti Nikola" (St. Nicholas of Myra in Lycia: honored December 6th). Nikola was the first-born of Dragomir and Katarina, who had eight other children, all of whom unfortunately perished later during World War II. The baptism of young Nikola took place in Ćelije Monastery, and was performed by beloved "Pop Andrija" (Fr. Andrew), the parish priest of the Serbian Orthodox Church in Lelić.

Nikola's parents were pious farmers who always interrupted their work schedule for daily prayer, which included keeping the yearly fasting routine as well as the liturgical cycle of the Orthodox Church. His mother, Katarina, quite pious and truly a holy woman, provided Nikola with his first lessons about God, Jesus Christ, the lives of the saints, and the holy days of the Church year. Often Nikola was seen being led by the hand of his mother to Ćelije Monastery—a walk of three miles—for prayer and Holy Communion. Later Nikola (as Bishop Nikolai) recalled these lessons on God and "walks with my mother" as being some of the most influential experiences in his life. He wrote of them in an autobiographical poem, written in Serbian, entitled "Prayers of a Captive in Prison" (1952).

Bishop Nikolai with his mother, Katarina, in front of his hometown church, Lelić, 1932.

Nikola's formal education began in Ćelije Monastery, dedicated to the Holy Archangels Michael and Gabriel, where his father, Dragomir, had hoped he "would learn to read the call to service from the government," in order to be a leading man and protector of his village, Lelić. "Pop Andrija" taught "mali Nikola" (Little Nicky), as he was known in Lelić, his first lessons in reading, writing, and mathematics. Besides these lessons, Fr. Andrew, being Nikola's spiritual father, taught him about the Scriptures and the teachings of the early Fathers of the Church, as well as the religio-national traditions of his Serbian heritage. This latter education was inspiring to Little Nicky from the very beginning. He demonstrated, even as a youngster, a tremendously penetrating mind and a zeal for learning. Quite often during summer breaks, Nikola would climb the bell tower of the catholicon (main church) of Ćelije Monastery and hide there all day long, occupying himself with prayer and the reading of books. Thus, with the influence of his mother, Katarina, and the lessons of beloved "Pop Andrija," Nikola seemed headed for far more than just being a leading citizen of his small village of Lelić. After finishing sixth grade in grammar school in Valjevo, Nikola petitioned for entrance into the Military Academy. However, he could not pass the physical exam, as he was, in the words of the physical fitness commission, "too small, not having large enough shoulders and a frame strong enough for such activities." This was certainly the divine will of our Heavenly Father, Who desired that Nikola travel on another path— to be a soldier of the Heavenly Kingdom and not of an earthly one. Immediately thereafter, Nikola applied for entrance into the Seminary of St. Sava in Belgrade, where he was accepted to begin studies as a seminarian. Besides studying the usual subjects, Nikola began reading the significant texts of the most famous writers of Western and Eastern European culture: Shakespeare, Voltaire, Nietzsche, Marx, Pushkin, Tolstoy, Dostoevsky, and others. His favorite author was without a doubt the Montenegrin Peter Njegoš, whose writings he had been reading since his early school days in Valjevo. His final examination for seminary studies was a discourse on the poetry and thought of Njegoš. This discussion, held in 1902 in Rakovica Monastery, located just ten miles south of Belgrade, amazed not only his fellow students, but his professors and instructors as well.

Life was difficult for Nikola during his years as a seminarian in Belgrade. Because of his poor eating habits and the terrible living conditions of the Seminary's housing facilities, Nikola contracted scrofula, a disease affecting the body's glands. After his seminary days, Nikola taught for a short while in the villages of Dračić and Leskovac, as well as in Valjevo. In Valjevo he befriended Fr. Sava Popović, whom he helped in parish activities, and from whom he "learned the ropes" of being involved with the faithful on an everyday basis. During summer breaks, at the advice of his doctor, Nikola spent time on the sea coast. It was during these "resting times" that he wrote the life of Bokel the Montenegrin and Dalmatian. Also at this time, Nikola founded a newspaper, *Hrišćanski Vesnik (Christian News),* in which appeared his first writings and articles.

In 1905, with his astute knowledge and evangelical activities, Nikola was chosen, along with several other students, to continue studies in Russia or Western Europe. Nikola chose to study in Europe, in the Old Roman Catholic Theological Faculty at the University of Berne, Switzerland. Besides studies in Berne, Nikola studied in Germany, England and, later, in Russia. He was exposed to the finest education Western Europe had to offer. He even became knowledgeable in the spiritual and philosophical books of ancient India. This learning made Nikola into a "Renaissance man," whose erudition and profundity of thought were considered by everyone as both a wellspring of knowledge and a unique treasury of wisdom and spirituality. In 1908, Nikola received his Doctorate in Theology in Berne, with the dissertation entitled *Faith in the Resurrection of Christ as the Foundation of the Dogmas of the Apostolic Church.* This original work was written in German, published in Switzerland, and later translated into Serbian. In the following year, 1909, this veritable genius, at age twenty-nine, prepared his Doctorate in Philosophy at Oxford, England; and during the summer of that same year in Geneva, Switzerland, Nikola wrote and defended his second doctoral dissertation, entitled *The Philosophy of Berkeley*, in French.

In the fall of 1909, Nikola returned home from Europe and became grievously ill from dysentery. This illness changed his life. Like the great theologian of the early Church, St. Gregory of Nazianzus (†390: honored January 25th and 30th), whose life was also dramatically changed through a personal difficulty,* Nikola decided to apply all his gifts and talents in service to God and His holy Orthodox Church. Lying in the hospital for over two months, Nikola prayed in his heart saying, "If my service to the Lord is needed, He will save me." He then vowed that if he returned to health he would become a monk and serve God's people in His Church. Thus as a Doctor in Theology and Philosophy, Nikola became the lowly monk Nikolai. After his tonsure into the monastic ranks, Monk Nikolai was ordained to the priesthood on the same day, December 20, 1909, in Rakovica Monastery. Hieromonk Nikolai now placed his entire being—his knowledge and all his talents—in the service of God and His Serbian Orthodox people; and within a short period of time, pious Fr. Nikolai was elevated to the rank of Archimandrite.

After his tonsure and ordination, Archimandrite Nikolai was chosen to be a teacher in the Seminary of St. Sava in Belgrade. However, it was discovered that he had not completed the final two years of gymnasium (grammar school), the seventh and eighth grades; he had to take a test in order to fulfill these requirements which would in turn validate his status as a teacher. The commission before whom Fr. Nikolai spoke was amazed with his wealth of insight. According to the words of one of its members, "Listening to his discourse on Christ, we were astonished, as no one could ask him one question or even say one word in reply." Yet it was decided that before Fr. Nikolai could become a teacher in the Seminary, he would be sent, with the blessing of Metropolitan Dimitrije of Serbia, to Russia. Spending over a year in Russia, Archimandrite Nikolai learned of the passionate Russian spirit and of the rich Orthodox soul of the peasantry. It was during this time that Blessed Nikolai wrote his first great work—*The Religion of Njegoš*. One of the contemporary critics said of this work that "from a religious-philosophical point of view, or a religiously critical point of view, the young seminary professor [Fr. Nikolai] is no less interesting than the Bishop of Cetinje [Njegoš]."

Returning to Belgrade as a seminary professor, Nikolai published, in 1912, an anthology of homilies entitled *Besede Pod Gorom (Sermons at the Foot of the Mount)*. Explaining the title, the humble Nikolai wrote, "Christ spoke on the Mount; I dare to speak only at the foot of the Mount." In 1914 Fr. Nikolai wrote the book *Iznad Greha i Smrti (Beyond Sin and Death)*, a writing of immense profundity yet with the ability to reach the soul of the common person.

---

* St. Gregory of Nazianzus' life was dramatically changed after the boat in which he was traveling from Athens to Cappadocia (Asia Minor) was wrecked in the Aegean Sea. He then vowed, if God desired him to be saved, to place all his talents in service of the Lord Jesus Christ and His Church.

Nikolai was most inspiring to his students. Under his spiritual influence and guidance, many went on to become monks, clergy, and theologians. One of them, Justin Popović, a spiritual disciple of Fr. Nikolai, became one of the greatest theologians in the history of the Serbian Orthodox Church (commemorated March 25th). Thus, besides teaching philosophy, logic, history, and foreign languages in Belgrade, the Rev. Dr. Nikolai Velimirović was fast becoming a great Serbian literary figure as well as a beloved spiritual pastor; soon, in addition, he would become a well-respected international figure.

With the outbreak of World War I in the summer of 1914, the entire Balkan Peninsula was thrown into turmoil. The imperiled Serbian nation badly needed a leader to help them survive this international crisis. To this end, Archimandrite Nikolai was called to embark upon an official diplomatic mission to England in order to obtain support from the

Bishop Elect Nikolai, 1919.

British government for the suffering Serbian people. Having received a doctorate from Oxford, Nikolai was received with honor and dignity by the British authorities. His political astuteness was revealed in several lectures and homilies delivered in England, which not only evoked a profound concern for the suppressed Serbs, but also addressed the issue of world peace and the methods to attain such a political ideal. Besides receiving British support for the Serbs, Nikolai was also personally awarded a Doctorate of

Divinity—honoris causa—from Cambridge University. His short tracts, "The Lord's Commandments" and "Meditations on the Lord's Prayer," electrified the Church of England, and also shattered many false conceptions of what the Orthodox Faith entailed.

In the late summer of 1915, Archimandrite Nikolai continued his "war mission" by traveling across the Atlantic Ocean to New York City. His mission was to rally the emigrant Serbs, Croats, and Slovenes against the Austrian government, for the majority of them had fled to America. His mission was quite successful, as America sent over 20,000 freedom-loving Slavic volunteers—called "the Third Army of Father Nikolai," most of whom fought on the Salonican Front—and hundreds of thousands of dollars worth of aid to their suffering brothers and sisters in the homeland. This trip was also quite revelatory for Nikolai: In a dream he received a message from an Angel of the Lord, who revealed to him that he would someday return to America and help organize the fledgling Serbian Orthodox communities into an American Serbian Diocese, totally united with the Dioceses in the motherland.

In early 1916 Nikolai returned to his beloved England where he decided to sojourn until the end of the war. He continued his literary activities by writing several articles and books: *The Religious Spirit of the Slavs* (1916—sent to the soldiers in the homeland); *Serbia in Light and Darkness* (1916); *The Serbian Soul, The Agony of the Church, The Serbian Orthodox Church,* and *The Spiritual Rebirth of Europe* (all in 1917). Oriented towards a British audience, these essays and books appealed to their sense of justice for suffering Serbia. In particular, *The Spiritual Rebirth of Europe* was of great interest to the Anglicans, for it promoted the possibility of a return of the Anglican Church to her rightful mother, the Orthodox Church. As a result of his academic excellence, Nikolai received another Honorary Doctorate of Divinity, in 1919, from the University of Glasgow in Scotland.

Feeling tremendously homesick, the patriotic Nikolai returned to Belgrade toward the end of the war. He then became involved in the formation of the new Yugoslav state as the interpreter for the then President of the government, Nikola Pašić. Yet Nikolai felt that there was something missing in his life. He wanted to be involved with his suffering people on a more daily basis. The fulfillment of this yearning came quickly: On March 12, 1919, the Holy Synod of the Serbian Orthodox Church selected Fr. Nikolai, at age 39, as the new Bishop of Žiča, the historical seat of the First Archbishopric of Serbia. During his episcopal consecration, Blessed Nikolai cried as a newborn babe in the Lord. Thus after four years of seeking support from England and America in behalf of Serbia, Bishop Nikolai was now ready to personally help in healing the war-torn hearts and souls of his beloved Serbian people.

For two years (1919–1921), Bishop Nikolai spiritually soothed pious Serbs not only in the Diocese of Žiča, but also throughout newly formed Yugoslavia. Imitating our Lord and Savior Jesus Christ,

Archpastor Nikolai "healed the sick, set free the spiritually captive, and preached salvation" to these humble souls. In 1921, Bishop Nikolai was transferred to the Diocese of Ohrid and Bitola. This was done to facilitate the union of the Serbian and Macedonian Churches which occurred as a result of the formation of the Kingdom of Yugoslavia. Blessed Father Nikolai, always a man of unity, peacefully engaged in the union of the Serbs and Macedonians of these regions. Besides sowing seeds of unity in his diocese, Nikolai also visited Athens, Constantinople, and the Holy Mountain, where he was received as a unifier of all Orthodox in the bond of love for Christ and His Church. During this time Nikolai wrote two books: *Reči o Svečoveku (Orations on the Universal Man:* 1920) and *Molitve Na Jezeru (Prayers by the Lake:* 1921). This latter work, written during his resting periods at Lake Ohrid, was in poetic-prose style, so deep and profound, similar in spirituality to the great Psalms of David. Yet Bishop Nikolai was not destined to stay in his homeland. Like a "beacon set upon a hill," his divine radiance was seen from afar, as he was invited to deliver lectures at various universities and Anglican Churches in America. At first, the Royal Government of the Kingdom of Yugoslavia as well as the Holy Synod of Bishops refused these requests for Bishop Nikolai; but the invitations kept coming so that, in the end, they both resolved to send beloved Nikolai to America for a second time.

On January 24, 1921, blessed Bishop Nikolai arrived, by the grace of God, in New York City. He had three immediate goals while in America: 1) to deliver lectures and homilies in universities and churches with the purpose of presenting World War I from the Eastern European viewpoint, 2) to collect funds for the setting up of orphanages in Serbia for those poor children who lost parents and relatives during World War I and, 3) to visit many Serbian Orthodox communities in order to thank them for their patriotic war efforts, along with making a report on the possibility of creating an American Serbian Diocese of the Serbian Orthodox Church.

The brilliant Bishop Nikolai was successful in all three phases of his mission. He delivered approximately 150 lectures and homilies in the following months. He spoke at a variety of places including Columbia University in New York City, various Serbian communities, and even the African-American community, speaking at St. Philip's Episcopal Church in Harlem, New York, to

St. Philip's Episcopal Church, Harlem, NYC.

some 1,500 parishioners. Wherever he spoke concerning the past World War, his message was clear. Do not blame the (Eastern) European peasant for the war, he proposed, but rather, look to the artificially created intel-

lectual class of the European university system. He wrote, "The European peasant is a noble spirit, but it is the intellectuals in charge of the peasants who are on the wrong track." Nikolai said that if these conditions in Western Europe continued, a second world war was likely to happen. And how right he was. One of his most enlightening sermons was delivered on the Sunday after Ascension, 1921, in the Episcopal Cathedral of St. John the Divine in New York City, entitled "The Stone which the Builders Rejected" (Mt. 21:42), in which he called for a return, on the part of Western Europe, to the true source and rock of their entire culture and civilization, to the Lord and Savior Jesus Christ, "the Way, the Truth, and the Life."

Nikolai also proposed that America, such a rich multi-national country, could possibly hold high the torch of hope for all of humankind. "The world has become small, but it waits to be proclaimed a united being. Europe has discovered the world. Can America organize it?" proclaimed Nikolai time and time again, with the hope that America would lead the way to a peaceful and just world for all. As a result of these speeches, Nikolai was called a "second Isaiah" and a "New Chrysostom" of our times; furthermore, his activities helped in obtaining acceptance of Yugoslavia into the League of Nations.

Concerning the development of orphanages for suffering Serbians both in the United States and Yugoslavia, Nikolai was motivated by the commandments of the Lord Jesus Christ: *Let the children come unto Me, and do not hinder them; for of such is the Kingdom of Heaven* (Mt. 19:14). *Take heed that ye despise not one of these little ones; for I say unto you, that in heaven their angels do always behold the face of my Father which is in heaven* (Mt. 18:10). *Come unto me, all ye that labor and are heavy laden, and I will give you rest. ... For my yoke is easy, and my burden is light* (Mt. 11:28, 30). *For I was an hungered, and ye gave me meat: I was thirsty, and ye gave me drink: I was a stranger and ye took me in: Naked, and ye clothed me. I was sick, and ye visited me: I was in prison, and ye came unto me. ... Verily ... inasmuch as ye have done it unto one of the least of these my brethren, ye have done it unto me* (Mt. 25:35-36, 40). Nikolai felt the pain of the loss of beloved ones so acutely that he often broke into tears upon visiting orphans and the poorest of the poor in his homeland. Prior to coming to America he set up an orphanage in Bitola, placing at its head the exiled Abbess Anna—previously known as the social worker Nada Adžić—in Vraćevšina Monastery. To the poor children in Yugoslavia, Bishop Nikolai became known as "Deda Vladika" (Grandfather Bishop), as one who really cared and "practiced what he preached" to alleviate their plight and difficulties. As head of the Council of Serbian Child Welfare in Belgrade, Nikolai, while in America, secured thousands of dollars for the cause of taking care of "these little ones." With this money he personally organized and supervised orphanages in Kraljevo, Čačak, Gornji Milanovac, and Kragujevac, where over 600 poor children were granted the love of Christ in personal social action.

Finally, concerning the creation of an American Serbian Diocese of the Serbian Orthodox Church, Bishop Nikolai wrote a Paschal Epistle in 1921 to all the Serbian Orthodox parishes in America. Blessed Nikolai extended greetings from the re-established Patriarchate of Serbia, from His Holiness Dimitrije, Patriarch of the Serbian Orthodox Church. He also outlined plans for the establishment of a Serbian Diocese in America. Nikolai, being the first Serbian hierarch ever to travel in America, was greeted with utmost respect upon visiting the Serbian communities. The problems of the Serbs in America were many: they were often pastored by Russian priests who did not understand their language; there were no monasteries to lead the people in the spiritual life; there was no seminary for education of clergy and the faithful; mixed marriages created confusion among the faithful; schisms in other Orthodox jurisdictions created a general mistrust of leadership among all Orthodox in America; Protestant and Roman Catholic church practices, as well as American secularism, were creeping into the life of the churches; and, above all, a lack of organization among the Serbian parishes made the Serbs feel like "an island in a great ocean." In the words of a letter of a Pittsburgh clergyman, sent to the Patriarch in early 1921, the Serbs in America were like "bees in a hive without a queen bee."

Bishop Nikolai returned to Belgrade on June 16, 1921, after six months of missionary activities in America. When he left, the American Serbians mourned the loss, but they all hoped that he would return as their new Bishop of the American Diocese. Yet this was not the will of the Lord. Ten days later, on June 26th, he gave his report on the American situation in a session of the Synod of Bishops held in Sremski Karlovci; and on September 21st, Metropolitan Varnava nominated Bishop Nikolai to assume the duties of Bishop of America, with Archimandrite Mardarije Uskoković of Rakovica Monastery (south of Belgrade) as his administrative assistant. This decision upset many pious Orthodox Serbs in the homeland, as none of them—bishops, clergy, monastics, and faithful—were ready to relinquish their beloved "Serbian Chrysostom" and evangelical leader to the American Serbs. Somewhat frustrated over this situation, in January of 1922, Bishop Nikolai went on a pilgrimage to the Holy Land, then traveled to the Holy Mountain, to Hilandar Monastery, to spend Pascha with the monks there. This sojourn was a spiritual necessity for Bishop Nikolai, as he retreated from the pressing problems and sought counsel from his Heavenly Father.

Upon his return for the gathering of the Synod of Bishops, Nikolai was convinced that the American situation needed a full-time bishop to carry out the ecclesiastical plans which the Angel of the Lord had previously revealed to him in his dream. Thus he, himself, nominated Archimandrite Mardarije Uskoković to be the future first permanent Bishop of the Serbian Orthodox Church in America. This nomination was confirmed by the entire Synod of Bishops, and on October 18, 1923, Archimandrite Mardarije was appointed the sole administrator of the Serbian Church in America. This decision was not only a spiritual blessing for Bishop Nikolai himself—relieving him of some of the many duties forced upon him—but it was also a divine blessing for the pious Serbs in the homeland. Nikolai was now able to devote himself fully to writing inspiring works as well as pastoring his faithful to be more fully immersed in the love of Jesus Christ and His Church. In 1923, Nikolai wrote *Nove Besede Pod Gorom (New Sermons at the Foot of the Mount)*, *Misli o Dobru i Zlu (Thoughts on Good and Evil)*, and a lengthy work entitled, *Omilije na Nedeljna i Praznična Evandjelja (Homilies on the Sunday and Festal Gospels)*.

Besides writing, Nikolai began a popular religious movement, later affectionately called *Bogomoljački Pokret (Movement of God-Prayers)*.* The venerable bishop's disciples loved to gather at his episcopal residence to sing the very moving and edifying songs he had written. Praising the Lord in their mother tongue was a joy and delight to these zealous Orthodox Serbs. The once-maligned Serbian Christians experienced in Nikolai an evangelical freshness which renewed their spirits after the war, and which allowed them to once again be fully immersed in the love of Jesus. By praying to the Lord in the vernacular Serbian, these Serbs, desirous of a fuller Christian life, were able to be built up into a people of God with the God-praising Nikolai leading the way. There were many priests who were jealous of Nikolai's "Bogomoljački Pokret," but as they began to experience the spiritual growth among their parishioners, they slowly supported this prayer movement. These Orthodox Serbian zealots—by their constant reading of the Scriptures, singing of spiritual songs, quickness of prayer, travels from monastery to monastery, regular confession of their sins, keeping of the fasts, and frequent communing of the precious Body and Blood of Jesus Christ—began to slowly transform the clergy of the various Serbian Dioceses. Bishop Nikolai, a master at pastoring his people, allowed his passionate God-seekers to lead the way in renewing the Serbian Church. Through this prayer movement, monasticism was revitalized as well as the study of theology, as was clearly

---

* This has also been rendered the "Devotionalist" or "Christian People's" Movement. [St. Xenia Editors.]

evidenced, for example, in the life of the great theologian and ascetic, Archimandrite Justin Popović of blessed memory.

In 1927, at the invitation of the American Yugoslav Society, the Institute of Politics in Williamstown, Massachusetts, and the Carnegie Endowment for International Peace, Bishop Nikolai once again traveled to America for his third visit. He spent only three months in America, speaking at various universities and churches as well as inquiring into the progress of the St. Sava Serbian Orthodox Monastery in Libertyville, Illinois, under the direction of newly consecrated Bishop Mardarije. On his way home to Serbia, Nikolai stopped in London where he stayed for two weeks, prophesying that an impending catastrophe was threatening Europe. The Prophet Nikolai, a man rooted in the present with a clear vision of the future, was a "voice crying in the wilderness" to a people in search of hope for a peaceful future. His message was clear: "Repent, for the Kingdom of God is at hand!"

Returning to Ohrid, the venerable bishop began writing once again. It seemed as though his sojourns in foreign lands filled his mind and heart—his total being—with restless divine thoughts of the promised Eternal Paradise; and the only way to relieve himself of these majestic longings was to write of them. In 1928 he wrote *Vera Obrazovanih Ljudi (The Faith of Educated People)*, *Rat i Biblija (War and the Bible)* and *Ohridski Prolog (The Prologue of Ohrid)*. This last book, over 1,000 pages, was patterned after ancient hagiographical literature which included both brief Lives and edifying incidents from the lives of holy men and wom-

St. John the Theologian Church in Ohrid, on the cliff overlooking Kaneo Beach.

en, as well as ordinary sinners. Also entitled *Žitija Svetih (The Lives of the Saints)*, this text was based upon the daily calendar of Orthodox Saints. Translated into English in 1985, *The Prologue of Ohrid* has become a spiritual classic to all Christians living in the West. The Bishop of Montenegro, Amfilohije Radović, a disciple of Nikolai, once said that "the only two books one needs to digest and put into practice to obtain salvation are the Bible and *The Prologue of Ohrid*."

In the town of Bitola in Bishop Nikolai's diocese was the Serbian Seminary of St. John the Theologian. From 1929 to 1934, one of the theology instructors there was the young Hieromonk John Maximovitch, the future Archbishop John. Bishop Nikolai valued and loved Fr. John, and exerted a beneficial influence upon him. More than once he was heard to say, "If you wish to see a living saint, go to Bitola to Fr. John." The lives of Bishop Nikolai and Fr. John would one day parallel each other: Both of them would spend the last years of their lives in America and die there, and both would be canonized as saints.*

---

* This paragraph has been added by the St. Herman of Alaska Brotherhood Editors from the Prima Vita of Archbishop John Maximovitch by Fr. Seraphim Rose.

In early 1930, Bishop Nikolai participated in the Pan-Orthodox Conference held at Vatopedi Monastery on the Holy Mountain. It can be said that Bishop Nikolai was "the Voice of Orthodoxy" during this time, as he was not only able to lead pious Orthodox Greeks, Serbs, Russians, and Bulgarians to transcend any nationalistic tendencies which might threaten the "bond of love" and "unity of spirit" among them; but also, perhaps more importantly, the venerable bishop, by his ability to abstract the true Holy Orthodox Tradition from all local Orthodox Church traditions, was able to present to Western Christians in a precise and comprehensive manner the true and eternal faith of the One, Holy, Catholic and Apostolic Church.

Bishop Nikolai arrested by the Germans, Žiča Monastery, 1941.

Prior to World War II, Nikolai wrote *Simvoli i Signali (Symbols and Signs:* 1932) and *Nomologija (Nomology,* i.e., *The Science of Law:* 1940) and, in 1937 until the outbreak of war in 1941, Nikolai began a compilation of his letters entitled *Misionarska Pisma (Missionary Letters).* This anthology of hundreds of letters witnessed to the amazing evangelical activity of Bishop Nikolai, as he was uniquely attuned to the spiritual crises of these perilous times.

In 1941, with the German occupation of Yugoslavia, Bishop Nikolai, together with Patriarch Gavrilo Dožić, was arrested and sentenced to imprisonment in the infamous Dachau Prison Camp in Germany. He spent two years in Dachau, witnessing and suffering some of the cruelest torture of human beings the world has ever known. Nikolai attributed his survival of this terrible ordeal to the Virgin Mary. While in prison, he wrote *Molbeni Kanon i Molitva Presvetoj Bogorodici (Supplicatory Canon and Prayers to the Most Holy Mother of God),* along with *Tri Molitve u Senci Nemačkih Bajoneta (Three Prayers in the Shadow of the German Bayonets)* which reads as a spiritual diary of his captive years. On May 8, 1945, as a result of the freedom secured by the 36th American Division of the Allied Forces, holy confessors Nikolai and Gabriel were released from prison. They both then sought sanctuary in England. Afterwards, the confessor Gabriel returned to Belgrade as patriarch, while the confessor Nikolai moved on to America for the fourth and final time. After recuperating from an aching back and leg problems, the exiled bishop began lecturing, as usual, in various educational institutions. In June of 1946 he was awarded, for his academic excellence, his final Doctorate of Sacred Theology from Columbia

University. In all, Bishop Nikolai obtained five doctorates.

From 1946 to 1949, Venerable Nikolai, always loyal to his Serbian people, taught at the St. Sava Seminary in Libertyville, Illinois. Realizing the need for American-born Serbians to have an Orthodox catechism in English, he published *The Faith of the Saints* (1949). In 1950 he wrote an essay on Orthodox mysticism in English, *The Universe as Signs and Symbols,* and a book in Serbian entitled, *Zemlja Nedodjija (The Unattainable Land)*. In 1951, his last book written while teaching at St. Sava's was, fittingly, *The Life of St. Sava.* According to the words of the distinguished professor Dr. Veselin Kesich, this book "reveals something about [Bishop Nikolai] himself in his meditation on the end of St. Sava's Life: 'Sava withdrew to his House of Silence in Studenica and offered a prayer to God "to let him die in a foreign country."' Why did he pray for this? Bishop Nikolai considers several reasons: Sava's protest against political disorder at home, his appeal to the conscience of his people, and his conviction that he would work for their salvation from the outside. These three reasons probably influenced the bishop's decision to come to America and not to return to Yugoslavia after the war."

In 1951, beloved Bishop Nikolai moved to St. Tikhon's Russian Orthodox Monastery in South Canaan, Pennsylvania. Here he spent the last five years of his earthly life as a professor, dean and, eventually, rector of the Seminary. Being all things to all people, Nikolai published articles in Russian for the God-seekers at St. Tikhon's. His ease and facility with languages was amazing to all. Nikolai could read, write, and speak fluently seven different languages.

Besides his activities at St. Tikhon's, Bishop Nikolai lectured at St. Vladimir's Seminary in Crestwood, New York, as well as at the Russian Orthodox Seminary and Monastery of the Holy Trinity in Jordanville, New York. Yet he did not forget his Serbian flock, as he published, in 1952, *Žetve Gospodnje (The Harvests of the Lord)* and *Kasijana (Cassiana),* a story of a penitent. In 1953, he wrote *Divan (Conversations),* a book on the "Bogomoljci" and their miracles. His final book, *Jedini Čovekoljubac (The Only Lover of Mankind)* was published posthumously in 1958. Bishop Nikolai's final undertaking was the Serbian Bible Institute, which published a series of seven short tracts on various theological topics: "Christ Died for Us," "Meditations on Seven Days," "Angels Our Elder Brethren," "Seven Petitions," "Bible and Power," "Missionary Letters," and "The Mystery of Touch."

Our holy and God-bearing father, Bishop Nikolai of blessed memory, fell asleep in the Lord while in prayer during the night between the 17th and 18th of March, 1956, in his humble cell at St. Tikhon's Russian Orthodox Seminary. He was 76 years old. He was given an honorable Orthodox Christian burial service in St. Sava Serbian Orthodox Cathedral in New York City, as pious Christians from all parts of the world came to hear eulogies in honor of one of the greatest hierarchs of the entire Orthodox Church in the twentieth century. From New York City his life-giving body was transferred to Libertyville, Illinois, just north of Chicago, to St. Sava Serbian Orthodox Monastery, where more Pomeni (memorial services) were held. He was laid to rest on the south side of the monastery church, on March 27, 1956.

Like St. Sava, the Enlightener of Serbia, holy Bishop Nikolai died in a foreign land. Behind the main church of Ćelije Monastery in his home village of Lelić, next to the grave of Archimandrite Justin Popović of blessed memory (†1979), was marked a place for his return to the homeland and the people he so very much loved. Thus, on April 27, 1991, after twenty-five years of repose in the Lord in America, holy Bishop Nikolai's body was returned to his homeland in Western Serbia. Pious American Orthodox, particularly many Russian Orthodox, did not forget the blessed Nikolai, as at St. Tikhon's Monastery his room was made into a shrine for prayer and meditation. His beloved disciple, Justin Popović, wrote these words in 1961, at the fifth anniversary of Blessed Nikolai's repose in the Lord: "Thank you, Lord—in him we have a new Apostle! Thank you, Lord—in him we have a new Evangelist! Thank you, Lord—in him we have a new Confessor! Thank you, Lord—in him we have a new Martyr! Thank you, Lord—in him we have a new Saint!"

EPILOGUE: In honor of St. Nikolai's glorification, his relics were exhumed and placed in a plain wooden reliquary in Lelić, in a church that St. Nikolai himself had built as the center of a men's monastery. The church is dedicated to St. Nicholas of Myra. More recently the reliquary has been replaced with one that, by its elaborate carving and full-length icon inside the lid, more fully expresses the love and devotion of pious people for him.* And St. Justin, next to whom he had been buried, was also exhumed for his glorification. His relics were translated back to Ćelije Monastery where

St. Nicholas of Myra Church in the Lelić Monastery, housing St. Nikolai's relics.

he had served God for the last three decades of his life. The two monasteries are not far apart, allowing pilgrims to readily venerate both Saints.

Prayer by St. Justin

O HOLY FATHER NIKOLAI, the magnificence of thy glory shines forth for all to see, as thy divine brilliance illumines us all with the superabundant love of Christ the Prince of Peace and Humble Shepherd. Pray to Christ the only Lover of Mankind, O most loving Arch-shepherd, for us weak and decrepit sinners, that His mind, His brilliance, His care, His energy, His divinity, His strength, His sacrifice, His humility and His resurrected glory may shine within our hearts so that we may in some small way spread His love to the ends of the earth. For to Him belong glory, honor, and worship, together with His unoriginate Father and life-giving Spirit, now and ever and unto ages of ages. Amen.

IC XC
НИ КА

---

* See page vi above.

Service

TO THE HOLY AND GOD-BEARING HIERARCH
SAINT NIKOLAI VELIMIROVIĆ
BISHOP OF OHRID AND ŽIČA

Whose Memory the Holy Church Celebrates
on March 5/18 and April 20/May 3 (†1956)

GREAT VESPERS

We chant Blessed is the man, *the first antiphon*
On Lord I have cried: *8 stichera are sung: 4 in Tone 3*

OME ALL YE PEOPLES of the Orthodox faith, and let us join the choirs of heaven in praise of holy Hierarch Nikolai Velimirović, a new victor in Christ over the darkness of this age, son of great peace, for he who sought to learn all knowledge, attained to the wisdom of God and became in his life a new and living Gospel of Christ, written in sufferings, affliction and great love, and he gave his mighty voice as a river of doctrine to the Serbian people and to the peoples of every land and nation, calling all to the fullness of the love of Christ. *Twice*

Strong in the Word, thy voice was a fountain of refreshment before the throne of God and descending from such a height, thy words became

15

a mountain torrent, full of sweetness and purity to nourish the souls parched in the desert of this world.

Holy Hierarch Nikolai, do not reject our childish babbling, but receive with fatherly love these offerings of thy children, for though we are as slow of tongue and speech as the Prophet Moses, yet it is impossible that we should be without hymns to praise thee.

Other stichera in Tone 6

Holy father, draw near to us and warm us with the fire of thy love for God, for we are grown cold and hard with worldliness and want of grace. Help us and guide us that we too may learn to live the evangelic life with consequence. *Twice*

As a new Sava thou didst awaken thy people to the love of Christ, as a new Nicholas thou wast a victor over the darkness of our times, as a new Chrysostom thou didst feed all with the honey of God's word. Father us also holy Hierarch Nikolai and guide our steps to walk aright.

The enemy stirred up envies and slanders against thee, trying constantly to buffet and toss thee on the stormy seas of this life, but thou didst prove thy name, victor and son of great peace, for thou didst calmly walk on the waves of this sea enduring all for thy love of Christ.

Glory: Tone 2

With the beauty and abundance of thine evangelical labors thou hast shown thyself worthy to be called the golden-tongued, after St. John Chrysostom. And as thou didst emulate him in thine apostolic labors—preaching, exhorting, correcting and instructing as a prophet among thy people—so didst thou suffer as he did from the enemy's malice—from hostility, persecutions, imprisonment and dying in exile, far from thy homeland. Like Chrysostom thou didst return, victorious, to thine episcopal throne in thy relics, to be a blessing and consolation to thy flock, a diocese without boundaries, because Žiča, as the very heart of Serbia, pumps its lifeblood throughout the whole Church.

Both now: Dogmaticon in the same tone

The shadow of the law passed away when grace arrived; for, just as the bush wrapped in flame did not burn, so the Virgin gave birth and yet remained a Virgin. In place of the pillar of fire, the Sun of righteousness shone forth; instead of Moses, Christ is come, the Salvation of our souls.

Entrance. Prokimenon of the day. Three Readings:

THE READING FROM PROVERBS
(10:7, 6; 3:13–16; 8:6a, 32, 35, 4 12, 14, 17, 5–9; 22:21a, 19)

THE MEMORY of the just is praised, and the blessing of the Lord is upon his head. Blessed is the man who hath found wisdom, and the mortal who knoweth prudence. For it is better to traffic for her, than for treasures of gold and silver. And she is more valuable than precious stones; and no precious thing is equal to her in value. For length of existence and years of life are in her right hand; and in her left hand are wealth and glory: out of her mouth proceeds righteousness, and she carries law and mercy upon her tongue. Hearken to me, O children, for I will speak solemn truths. Blessed is the man who shall keep my ways; for my outgoings are the outgoings of life, and in them is prepared favour from the Lord. You, O men, I exhort; and utter my voice to the sons of men. I, wisdom, have dwelt with counsel and knowledge, and I have called upon understanding. Counsel and safety are mine; prudence is mine, and strength is mine. I love those that love me; and they that seek me shall find grace. O ye simple, understand subtlety, and ye that are untaught, imbibe knowledge. Hearken to me; for I will speak solemn truths; and will produce right sayings from my lips. For my throat shall meditate truth; and false lips are an abomination before me. All the words of my mouth are in righteousness; there is nothing in them wrong or perverse. They are all evident to those that understand, and right to those that find knowledge. I therefore teach thee truth, that thy hope may be in the Lord, and that ye may be filled with the Spirit.

THE READING FROM PROVERBS
(10:31–11:12)

THE MOUTH of the righteous drops wisdom: but the tongue of the unjust shall perish. The lips of just men drop grace: but the mouth of the ungodly is perverse. False balances are an abomination before the Lord: but a just weight is acceptable unto him. Wherever pride enters, there will be also disgrace: but the mouth of the lowly meditates wisdom. When a just man dies he leaves regret: but the destruction of the ungodly is speedy, and causes joy. Righteousness traces out blameless paths: but ungodliness encounters unjust dealing. The righteousness of upright men delivers them: but transgressors are caught in their own destruction. At the death of a just man his hope does not perish: but the boast of the ungodly perishes. A righteous man escapes from a snare, and the ungodly man is delivered up in his place. In the mouth of ungodly men is a snare to citizens: but the understanding of righteous men is prosperous. In the prosperity of righteous men a city prospers: but by the mouth of ungodly men it is overthrown. A man void of understanding sneers at his fellow citizens: but a sensible man is quiet.

THE READING FROM THE WISDOM OF SOLOMON
(4:7–15)

BUT THOUGH the righteous be prevented with death, yet shall he be in rest. For honourable age is not that which standeth in length of time, nor that is measured by number of years. But wisdom is the gray hair unto men, and an unspotted life is old age. He pleased God, and was beloved of him: so that living among sinners he was translated. Yea speedily was he taken away, lest that wickedness should alter his understanding, or deceit beguile his soul. For the bewitching of naughtiness doth obscure things that are honest; and the wandering of concupiscence doth undermine the simple mind. He, being made perfect in a short time, fulfilled a long time: for his soul pleased the Lord: therefore hasted he to take him away from among the wicked. This the people saw, and understood it not, neither laid they up this in their minds, that his grace and mercy is with his saints, and that he hath respect unto his chosen.

At the Litia: Sticheron of the temple,
then of the Saint, in Tone 6

From Lelić to South Canaan, from Žiča to Harlem, from Ohrid to London and to Libertyville, thou didst follow in the steps of the apostles, holy Nikolai. As a citizen of heaven and peer of saints and angels, thou didst walk through the shadow of death, facing horrors unknown till our time. And always thou didst shine the lamp of evangelical love and forgiveness as thou didst search amidst the dust and dross of this age, for the lost coin: the image of God in the human soul. Guide us also to walk aright and discern the dangers and needs of our times.

Glory: in the same Tone

Armed with the peace from above, thou didst war against powers and principalities, against the darkness of this age, confronting its horrors with the meekness of Christ. Thine all-powerful weapons were love and forgiveness for those who attacked and persecuted thee, and an all-daring trust in God. Thou didst overpower the malice of the evil one, as Christ's victor in battle, O holy Hierarch Nikolai.

Both now: Theotokion in the same Tone

O comforter of the afflicted and seeker of the lost, thou didst support our Father Nikolai through many grievous trials and sorrows; comfort and guide us also in our journey that we may bravely endure the saving sufferings allowed to us.

Aposticha, Tone 6
To the special melody: Having laid aside

THE GRACE of thy life and labors did reverberate from Sava's Žiča to bring about a spiritual rebirth to all the Serbian peoples as thou didst teach that to perform the Church's services is to work miracles, and so thou didst perform the services with care as a new wonderworker.

Verse: Precious in the sight of the Lord *is the death of His saints.*

As an exile thou didst prove thine apostolic calling, for as the Gospel was spread by the early Christians when they fled persecutions in Jerusalem, so thy teachings did reach many new peoples through the malice and machinations of the enemy.

Verse: What shall I render to the Lord *for all His benefits toward me?*

With thy vigils, prayers and weeping, holy Hierarch Nikolai, thou didst intercede for the whole world, praying for friends and neighbors and even for thine enemies whom thou didst call thy "cruel friends" and with thy pen thou didst pour forth a torrent of prayer and teaching in thy great compassion and love for souls.

Glory: in the same Tone

O man of holy wisdom and grace, ever sacrificing thyself for the Gospel of Love, healing hearts and souls of those wounded in their struggles, lifting up the fallen and supporting the weak, father of many orphans, thou didst provide light for a darkened world, leading many with great labor to heavenly repose.

Both now: Theotokion in the same Tone

My Creator and Redeemer, O most pure one, Christ the Lord, having come forth from thy womb and become clothed in flesh like mine, hath delivered Adam from the primal curse. Wherefore to thee, O most pure one, as Mother of God and Virgin, we cry out ceaselessly in truth: Rejoice like the angels, rejoice, O Sovereign Lady, intercession and protection and salvation of our souls.

Troparion from Fr. Daniel Rogich, in Tone 8 (twice)

LOVING THY HOMELAND thou didst sojourn as a patriot to secure aid for God's suffering children, and as a new Chrysostom thou didst preach to those in darkness the rediscovery of the Foundational Rock, Christ the Lord, in the eternal homeland of God's Kingdom; thy pastoral love for all, O Confessor Nikolai, was purified in captivity by the godless, demonstrating thy commitment to the truth and to thy people, therefore O venerable hierarch, thou hast attained the crown of eternal life.

O Theotokos and Virgin, rejoice *(once)*

MATINS

On God is the Lord, *Troparion of the Saint twice.*
Glory, Both now: Resurrectional Theotokion

THOU WHO FOR OUR SAKE wast born of a Virgin and didst suffer crucifixion, O Good One, and didst despoil death by death, and reveal the resurrection as God: Despise not those whom Thou hast fashioned with Thine own hand, reveal Thy love for mankind, O Merciful One, accept the intercession for us of the Mother of God who gave birth to Thee, and save, O our Saviour, a despairing people.

After the first kathisma, Sedalion in Tone 2

"The Cross and freedom are two words for the same thing" —so thou didst teach thy spiritual children, "because real freedom is found only in the religion of the Cross." Help us also, holy Hierarch Nikolai, to embrace the Cross in our lives and so achieve this true freedom. *(Twice)*

Glory, Both now: Theotokion

Our Lady Theotokos, Mother of all our joy, guide us toward our heavenly homeland through the joyful embrace of difficulties.

After the second kathisma, Sedalion in Tone 2

Thou didst bring thy people their first renewal from the time of St. Sava—teaching them once again to be Christ-bearers—and didst lead them through the valley of the shadow of death with courage, renewing their faith and love for Christ in an ocean of sorrows. Then thou didst bring to the West the deep wisdom of the Cross. *(Twice)*

Glory, Both now: Theotokion

Most Holy Theotokos, thou unburnt bush before which the Prophet Moses removed his shoes, enkindle an unquenchable love in our hearts that we may also leave behind the worn-out shoes of our worldly understanding and come before thy Son with the daring of deep love.

Polyeleos, and Megalynarion

We magnify thee, O holy Hierarch Nikolai, and we honor thy holy memory, for thou dost pray for us to Christ our God.

Selected Psalm verse:
Hear this, all ye nations; give ear, all ye that inhabit the world (Ps. 48:1).

After the Polyeleos, Sedalion in Tone 2

Holy Father Nikolai, thou hast wandered over the earth as a new apostle, and spread the Gospel to all peoples as an evangelist and didst reach many more with thy comfort and love through thy writings. As a new confessor thou didst witness to Christ in the darkest places of the world and finally completed thy contest as a new martyr. Strengthen us also, through thy prayers to bear witness to Christ and His Church, in all the paths on which He leads us.

Glory, Both now: Theotokion

O Lady Mother of God, ray of the spiritual sun that doth light our path and guide our way through the trials of this world, intercede with thy Son and our God that in His mercy He may ever draw us to Himself and save us.

Hymn of Ascents, the first antiphon of Tone 4: From my youth

Prokimenon, in Tone 4

My mouth shall speak of wisdom, *and the meditation of my heart shall be of understanding.*

Verse: Hear this, all ye nations: give ear, all ye that inhabit the world.

Let every breath praise the Lord.

THE READING FROM THE HOLY GOSPEL ACCORDING TO ST. JOHN, § 35 FROM THE MIDPOINT (John 10:1–9)

THE LORD SAID, to the Jews who came unto Him, "Verily, verily, I say unto you, He that entereth not by the door into the sheepfold, but climbeth up some other way, the same is a thief and a robber. But he that entereth in by the door is the shepherd of the sheep. To him the porter openeth; and the sheep hear his voice: and he calleth his own sheep by name, and leadeth them out. And when he putteth forth his own sheep, he goeth before them, and the sheep follow him: for they know his voice. And a stranger will they not follow, but will flee from him: for they know not the voice of strangers." This parable spake Jesus unto them: but they understood not what things they were which he spake unto them. Then said Jesus unto them again, "Verily, verily, I say unto you, I am the door of the sheep. All that ever came before me are thieves and robbers: but the sheep did not hear them. I am the door: by me if any man enter in, he shall be saved, and shall go in and out, and find pasture."

After Psalm 50, Sticheron, in Tone 6

As a true ambassador of the peace that is from above thou didst lead thy flocks through two world wars and terrible afflictions, and didst bring the true peace of Christ to foreign shores. Thus thou wast always embattled for bearing Christ, for preaching the Gospel, for living the Beatitudes, for forgiving thine enemies, for comforting those in sorrow and in all these things thou wast a true victor in Christ, proclaiming in the darkest regions, Christ the Conqueror of death.

Supplicatory Canon to the Theotokos, with 6 troparia, including the irmos, in Tone 8, and the Canon to the Saint with 8 troparia in Tone 2

ODE I

Irmos: Come, O ye people, let us sing a hymn to Christ our God, who divided the sea and guided the people whom He had led forth from Egyptian bondage, for He hath been glorified.

Refrain: Holy Hierarch Nikolai, pray to God for us.

O Lord, open my lips and enlighten the faculties of my soul to sing of Thy new Moses, who parted the waves of the seas to lead his people to safety and peace in the midst of the stormy waves of war and persecution.

Holy Hierarch Nikolai, golden-tongued, the honey of thy discourse has flooded our souls with the sweetness of Christ. Direct us now to seek our true freedom in the Cross of Christ.

Thou didst study and become one of the most educated men of thy time, steeped in both Western education and the wisdom of the East. After completing thy worldly education thou didst turn from it to school thy soul in a deeper wisdom, the radiant peasant piety of thy homeland.

Having received the best education that the world could offer, thou didst turn from it as from fool's gold and as poverty and deficiency, valuing in its place the wisdom of the Gospel and the piety of thy people.

Theotokion: Holy Lady and Mother of our God, thou golden jar of heavenly manna, thou didst teach our Father Nikolai how to nourish the people of God, wherefore we cry to thee, help us, save us, and lead us to our heavenly home.

Katavasia as prescribed by the Typicon.

ODE III

Irmos: Establish us in Thee, O Lord who hast slain sin by the Tree, and plant the fear of Thee in the hearts of us who hymn Thee.

Like the stone which the builders rejected thou wast turned away from the military academy because of thy small stature. Thus by God's providence thou wast preserved for a higher calling and a much greater stature, O holy Nikolai.

Lover of wisdom and beauty and truth, thou didst guide a spiritual fellowship of Christian people, using them to inspire piety and unity among all thy flock, and thy spiritual labors did spread from Žiča as from the very heart of Serbia to all lands and peoples, wherefore we praise thee and love thee, meek lamb and lion of Christ.

Receive our praises, loving father, as the lisping of young children, for we have not thy golden tongue to praise thee worthily, yet our love must have words of praise for thee.

Theotokion: O eastern door of the temple that has never been opened—thus showing an image of thine ever-virginity—pray for us, O Lady, that we too may learn to walk aright in this path set for us by thy Son.

Sedalion in Tone 6

With the greatness of deep humility, Hierarch Nikolai, thou didst place thyself at the foot of the mount from which Christ preached, in order to speak thy words. Thou didst not dare to lift thine eyes to its heights nor offer thyself as an authority. Thus thou didst preach with the authority of the Church and thy teachings soared as a fitting vessel for the wisdom of God.

Glory, Both now: Theotokion

More spacious than the heavens, thou didst contain the uncontainable God, higher than the heavens, thou didst provide His throne. Most humble of all thou didst not disdain the stable, the manger, the exile's journey, the sword-pierced heart. Most pure one, we cannot praise thee worthily but we bring thee a child's love.

Ode IV

Irmos: I hymn Thee, O Lord, for I heard report of Thee and I was afraid; for Thou comest to me seeking me who have strayed. Wherefore I glorify Thy great condescension toward me, O greatly Merciful One.

As a diplomat thou didst use thy great learning to seek aid for thy little Serbia, yet thou didst reject the cornerstone of Western education that man should be the measure of man, teaching instead the true cornerstone —Christ the Godman as humanity's only true measure.

Thine apostolic labors began in Žiča as thou didst weep with gratitude for the cross given thee, thus joining thee to the sufferings of thy flock, and thou didst carry this cross of true freedom through foreign lands, through wars, imprisonment and exile, never ceasing to preach the Gospel with thy golden words, in and out of season.

Deep calleth unto deep, holy God-seer Nikolai, and thou didst descend into the living hell of Dachau to understand the grave flaws in Western culture, and from there thou didst call upon the name of Christ until thou didst behold the face of God.

Theotokion: Most Holy Theotokos, thou didst carry thy holy Hierarch Nikolai, as in a boat, over the seas of blood and terror, caught in the worst wars we have yet seen. Carry us also, our Lady, to the safe harbor of thy Son.

Ode V

Irmos: O Lord, Bestower of light and Creator of the ages, guide us in the light of Thy commandments, for we know none other God than Thee.

How thou didst suffer, O holy Nikolai, because thine imprisonment cut thee off from the sufferings of thy people, for as a loving shepherd thou couldst not bear to be separated from the afflictions of thy flock.

How the enemy feared thee and sought to win thee over to cooperation with the invaders, but for thee there could be no compromise between light and darkness. And so thou wast transferred to the death camps from whence no human help could deliver thee.

Upon telling the Nazi guards of thy disbelief in God, they thought they had seized victory, but were utterly silenced by thy words: "I do not believe in God; I know Him!"

Theotokion: Most holy Lady, foreshadowed in the burning bush that Moses saw, teach us also to burn with the fervor of love for God.

Ode VI

Irmos: Whirled about in the abyss of sin, I call upon the unfathomable abyss of Thy loving kindness: Lead me up from corruption, O God.

Out of the deadly maw of Dachau, thou didst rise as a new Jonah from the belly of the leviathan, and as Jonah thou wast sent to preach to new Ninevites who knew not their right hand from their left.

Exile was a bitter draught for thee, holy Hierarch Nikolai, for once again thou wast separated from thy flock, but in truth thy flock grew beyond all boundaries. And we are so grateful that thou didst come to walk among us and feed us with the golden honey of thy teachings.

The generosity of thy noble heart was such that thou couldst always see the good, the noble, and the beautiful in all those thou didst meet. And thou didst cover over that which was lacking even in those who attacked thee.

Theotokion: Holy Lady, teach us also to use divine love as our measure in all our dealings with our neighbors that we, together with them may be led into a deeper love of God.

It is customary to sing the first kontakion and ikos from the Akathist and to resume Matins which continues on page 37.

AKATHIST
TO OUR HOLY HIERARCH NIKOLAI

Kontakion 1, in Tone 8

Born in Serbian Lelić, thou wast the archpastor of St. Naum's Ohrid. Thou didst preside from the throne of St. Sava in Žiča. By the Gospel thou didst instruct and enlighten the people of God. Thou didst lead many to repentance and love for Christ. For Christ's sake thou didst endure suffering in Dachau; for this O Saint, He glorified thee, Nikolai, universal teacher.

Ikos 1

As a heavenly man and fellow of the stars, O holy Hierarch Nikolai, thou didst even compose hymns for all the angelic orders, offering thy prayers with theirs to the Conqueror of death. How shall we who are dust and ashes dare to praise thee worthily, Nikolai the new God pleaser, as we sing:

Rejoice, holy shepherd of Serbia;
Rejoice, glorious apostle to the New World!
Rejoice, fiery pillar of love for God;
Rejoice, thou who hast borne the sufferings of thy people!
Rejoice, holy Hierarch Nikolai, universal teacher!

Kontakion 2

As a scion of the village of Lelić thou wast the first of nine children born to pious Christian peasants and didst receive thy first lessons in piety and love for God from thy holy mother, Katarina, as thou didst accompany her on the three-mile walk to Monastery Ćelije for prayers and Communion and there, with all thy heart thou didst first cry: Alleluia!

Ikos 2

As a small and weak child, thine elders doubted that thou couldst live to adulthood and believed that thou shouldst not be required to endure the hardships necessary to acquire an education, yet thy child's soul was hungry for learning and they did not have the heart to hold thee back. Thus didst thou become the most learned man in Serbia to whom we all cry:

Rejoice, for thou didst fathom all the wisdom of the world;

Rejoice, for thou hast acknowledged all secular learning as dross!

Rejoice, for thou hast sought the heavenly treasure;

Rejoice, for thou didst sell all for that pearl of great price!

Rejoice, holy Hierarch Nikolai, universal teacher!

Kontakion 3

Instead of playing childish games, thou didst prefer to climb the belfry of the Church and sit like an eagle in his eyrie, spending quiet hours there in prayer and reading, feeding thy hungry soul on the mysteries of God and His creation, and thus thou didst progress as St. Paul did at the feet of Gamaliel learning to cry: Alleluia!

Ikos 3

Thy frailty was allowed by God's Providence so that as the stone that the builders rejected thou wast denied entry into the military academy because of thy small stature, yet thou didst teach all to understand that God's strength is made perfect in weakness for thou wast called to serve in God's army, lifting thy prayers to heaven as a mighty intercessor before the throne of God. Wherefore we raise our cries to thee:

Rejoice, child of grace;
Rejoice, peer of the apostles!
Rejoice, secret treasury of the wisdom of God;
Rejoice, thou instrument of His providence!
Rejoice, holy Hierarch Nikolai, universal teacher!

Kontakion 4

Enduring the poor food and the cold and damp conditions at seminary, thou didst prepare thy many talents for God's service, and while undergoing voluntary labors for His love, thou didst also endure involuntary illness, learning patience in thy weakness. In all things thou didst gain wisdom as thou didst acquire the best education of thy times, understanding and integrating all thy studies by the lamp of God's Word as thou didst sing: Alleluia!

Ikos 4

Thou didst love the beauty and wisdom of Western education when thou didst study abroad, and yet as thou didst love its accomplishments, thou didst also come to see its failures and its darkness. Thou didst come to understand that it was naught but poverty and deficiency, lacking the true Cornerstone that such an education should have—Christ, our only true measure. Awed by thy teaching we cry to thee:
Rejoice, overflowing fountain of theology;
Rejoice, spiritual harp!
Rejoice, beloved heart of thy people;
Rejoice, apostle to the New World!
Rejoice, holy Hierarch Nikolai, universal teacher!

Kontakion 5

After acquiring doctorates in theology and philosophy thou didst suffer from illness and didst vow that thou wouldst serve Christ with thy life. Thus thou didst receive the monastic schema and ordination at Rakovica Monastery, placing all thy gifts with thy soul in God's hands to use as He chose as thou didst cry: Alleluia!

Ikos 5

Thou didst teach in St. Sava Seminary in Belgrade and didst truly begin thy ministry with lectures and orations throughout thy homeland, becoming the great golden bell of Serbia, calling all of its people to Church, spiritual renewal, and unity in Christ; wherefore we sing to thee:

Rejoice, holy melody of prayer;
Rejoice, new book of the wisdom of God!
Rejoice, eloquence of the Serbian soul;
Rejoice, sweet savor of the Gospel of Christ!
Rejoice, holy Hierarch Nikolai, universal teacher!

Kontakion 6

As a companion of saints and righteous ones thou didst know St. John Maximovitch when he was a young monk and didst tell others that if they wished to see a living saint they should look to him as thou didst cry: Alleluia!

Ikos 6

Thy teachings and thy prayers formed a new generation in the love of Christ as thou didst form thy followers into an army of prayer, crying out to God for the needs of the whole Church and for spiritual rebirth, so we sing:

Rejoice, new voice for the Wisdom of God;
Rejoice, instructor of His Providence!
Rejoice, new fountain of the Orthodox faith;
Rejoice, new well refreshing those who thirst!
Rejoice, holy Hierarch Nikolai, universal teacher!

Kontakion 7

Suffering with thy little Serbia, thou didst serve her as an ambassador during the Great War. After so many trials thou didst rebuke the British Parliament for negotiating a peace that was not blessed by the peace from above and thou didst bring them all to their knees to cry to the Holy Trinity: Alleluia!

Ikos 7

Thou didst ever bear the sufferings of thy people within thy heart, seeking to lighten their burdens, providing comfort, prayer, encouragement and rebuke, as a skilled physician. As a salve to heal the wounds of thy countrymen thou didst apply the medicines of prayer and teaching to lift them again to their heritage as servants of God. Heal us, also, that we may cry to thee:

Rejoice, new prophet for our times;
Rejoice, thou who didst pass through the abyss of misery as gold through the furnace!
Rejoice, thou who wast proved and weighed in deepest suffering and afflictions;
Rejoice, thou who didst endure all for the love of Christ!
Rejoice, holy Hierarch Nikolai, universal teacher!

Kontakion 8

The enemy of mankind greatly feared thine influence on thy flock and so contrived to keep thee isolated and imprisoned together with the patriarch at the beginning of the Second World War, but even this was not enough for him. So he sought to stir up calumny and persecution against thee, yet thou couldst not be moved to speak against those who attacked thee as thou didst cry: Alleluia!

Ikos 8

What wonder is this, that through the love of Christ, all the envy and scorn directed at thee could only be returned with love and mercy, and often with silence, covering the sins of those who wished thee every harm. We look upon thy labors and ask thee to help us also to learn such loving forbearance as we cry:

Rejoice, Nikolai, victor over the devil's enmity;
Rejoice, thou who didst lead by true example!
Rejoice, thou outpouring of the mercy of God;
Rejoice, for great is thy reward in heaven!
Rejoice, holy Hierarch Nikolai, universal teacher!

Kontakion 9

Because the Nazis could not turn thee to their use, they sent thee to Dachau, their death camp, hoping to drown thy voice and thy witness in that sea of hopelessness, but even this sorrow thou didst turn to the good with thy witness to the Truth and with thy holy prayers from the very nadir of thy suffering to the vision of God as thou didst cry: Alleluia!

Ikos 9

Thou didst reach such a depth of prayer in Dachau that later when asked about thy experience there, thou didst reply that if possible thou wouldst give the rest of thy life for another hour in Dachau for surely nothing else had brought thee so close to Christ, and we cry with amazement:

Rejoice, new David who didst praise God on the harp of the Beatitudes;

Rejoice, thou who didst ascend to heaven in the chariot of prayer!

Rejoice, for the myrrh of thy suffering has ascended before the throne of God;

Rejoice, now for all the sufferings thou hast borne for Christ!

Rejoice, holy Hierarch Nikolai, universal teacher!

Kontakion 10

Exiled from thy homeland as the first Christians were exiled from Jerusalem so that by God's Providence, the true faith might reach new lands and peoples, thou didst take up thine exile with apostolic zeal, eager only to teach, to serve, to bring the peace of Christ as thou didst cry: Alleluia!

Ikos 10

Bitterly thou didst suffer for thy people in thine exile, and often wouldst comfort thyself, playing folk music on a shepherd's pipe from thy homeland, and yet, as a shepherd of new flocks, thou didst play the true shepherd's pipe of the word of God to all who came to thee as they cried:

Rejoice, noetic flute of the Spirit;

Rejoice, melodious voice of the Gospel of Christ!

Rejoice, instrument of the Wisdom of God;
Rejoice, golden melody of truth!
Rejoice, holy Hierarch Nikolai, universal teacher!

Kontakion 11

As a comforter of the afflicted and apostle of freedom thou wast the first Orthodox hierarch to reach out to the African-American Christians of Harlem and as thou didst preach to them they gave thee their tribute, a standing ovation as they cried: Alleluia!

Ikos 11

As a scion of Serbia thou didst know how to console those downtrodden by injustice and tyranny and didst show how the children of St. Sava embraced a love for all peoples, never counting others as less than sons of God. Amazed by this we shout to thee:
Rejoice, melodious voice of the love of God;
Rejoice, trumpet of golden freedom!
Rejoice, heart enlarged by the Gospel of Christ;
Rejoice, Christ's victor in the New World!
Rejoice, holy Hierarch Nikolai, universal teacher!

Kontakion 12

Like St. John the golden-tongued thou didst die in exile, amidst thine apostolic labors, but the grief of thy loss was turned to joy for thy spiritual children, for even in death thy voice could not be silenced but rings throughout all Orthodox lands, calling all to worship the Holy Trinity in Orthodox manner as they cry: Alleluia!

Ikos 12

At last the door opened for the return of thy relics to thy homeland and through this event, the doors of heaven also opened with the grace to bring forgiveness and healing to thy peoples; for this was the beginning of healing for the Serbian Church, bringing together those parts rent by schism. Standing before thy grace-bearing relics we offer these hymns to thee:

Rejoice, new apostle to a darkened world;
Rejoice, herald of the Gospel of Christ!
Rejoice, presence of the Kingdom of God;
Rejoice, ambassador of the peace which is from above!
Rejoice, holy Hierarch Nikolai, universal teacher!

Kontakion 13

Holy Father Nikolai, Christ's victor over the darkness of this world both in life and after death, hear the prayers of thy children and lead and guide us upon the path of salvation. Help us to find our way in times of great darkness and affliction and be ever a light and a guide to us in our journey to the Heavenly Kingdom as we cry: Alleluia! *(Three times)*

Ikos 1

As a heavenly man and fellow of the stars, O holy Hierarch Nikolai, thou didst even compose hymns for all the angelic orders, offering thy prayers with theirs to the Conqueror of death. How shall we who are dust and ashes dare to praise thee worthily, Nikolai the new God pleaser as we sing:
Rejoice, holy shepherd of Serbia;
Rejoice, glorious apostle to the New World!
Rejoice, fiery pillar of love for God;
Rejoice, thou who hast borne the sufferings of thy people!
Rejoice, holy Hierarch Nikolai, universal teacher!

Kontakion 1

Born in Serbian Lelić, thou wast the archpastor of St. Naum's Ohrid. Thou didst preside from the throne of St. Sava in Žiča. By the Gospel thou didst instruct and enlighten the people of God. Thou didst lead many to repentance and love for Christ. For Christ's sake thou didst endure suffering in Dachau; for this O Saint, He glorified thee, Nikolai, universal teacher.

ODE VII

Irmos: When the golden image was worshipped on the plain of Dura, Thy three youths spurned the godless command, and cast into the midst of the fire, bedewed they sang: Blessed art Thou the God of our fathers!

The tintinnabulations of thy prayer and labors resounded from the heart of Serbia throughout the Orthodox world, calling all to prayer and spiritual rebirth, and to battle against the encroaching darkness.

In the time of great darkness, and unspeakable horror and loss, thou didst shine as a light on a hill, so that the enemy feared thee all the more in thy silence and imprisonment.

As thine enemies attacked and slandered thee, and labeled thee as enemy of the people, so did thy flock respond contrariwise with love, calling for thy return.

Theotokion: Most Pure Lady, Mother of God, thou didst shelter Hierarch Nikolai in the storms and the nadir of his grief—shelter us also so that we may not be crushed or defeated in our warfare for Christ.

ODE VIII

Irmos: God who descended into the fiery furnace for the Hebrew children and transformed the flame into dew, hymn ye as Lord, O ye works, and exalt Him supremely for all ages!

Thy Devotionalists became known as thine army and their prayer brought hope to the fallen and strengthened the faith of the Church.

Exiled from thy homeland, thou didst become a new apostle to a foreign land, reaching out to many who had not known the ancient Church.

Thy people's history of enslavement guided thy compassion as thou wast the first hierarch to preach to the African-American Christians of this land and, from the sufferings of thine own people, thou wast able to understand their suffering and bring succor.

The children followed after thee through Harlem for the candies in thy pocket and for thy loving prayer that they would also know our sweetest Jesus.

Theotokion: Most Holy Lady, thou didst strengthen thy golden-tongued Nikolai to sow the Gospel seed far and wide. Bless now the harvest of the many fields he sowed and bring forth laborers to this harvest for Christ's sake.

Ode IX

Irmos: O ye faithful, let us magnify with hymns in oneness of mind, the Word of God, who from God came in His ineffable wisdom, to renew Adam who had grievously fallen into corruption through eating, and who became ineffably incarnate of the holy Virgin for our sake.

Thou wast the first to teach Orthodox seminarians in English for the students who would serve as clergy in the American land, preparing them to preach the Gospel and serve in the language of the people.

The division of the Serbs in the new land was a grievous wound to thee, holy Hierarch Nikolai, but as thy relics were prepared for their return to Serbia, thou didst prove to be a peacemaker, bringing about forgiveness where there had been enmity.

O holy new apostle of love, for thine own people and for all peoples, receive our humble prayer and help us also to grow in love and forgiveness so that by thy prayers we may be made worthy to live with thee and with Christ forever.

Theotokion: O holy and living ark of our salvation, new Torah upon which the Word was written, shelter us through the trials and afflictions of this life, defend and intercede for all of us who call upon thy name.

Exapostilarion in Tone 3

As a bright star in the dark night of the latter times thou dost bring apostolic grace and the freedom of the Cross to all who seek to follow

Christ. Guide us now with thy wisdom and prayer to follow our Shepherd through every difficulty.

Glory, Both now: Theotokion

Gabriel greeted thee with awe, Most Holy Mother of God, for thou didst bear the Spiritual Sun that has enlightened our darkness and shines now in all of our hearts.

Praises, 4 stichera in Tone 5
To the special melody: Rejoice, life-giving Cross

BLESSED ARE THE MERCIFUL; and thou O Hierarch Nikolai, wast a chosen vessel of the mercy of Christ to thy flock and to all peoples, grieving with those who suffered, mourning with those who mourned in thy homeland and abroad, and didst care for the orphans and the destitute, becoming a consolation to all.

Blessed are they who hunger and thirst after righteousness; and thou, our Father Nikolai, didst put on the righteousness of Christ, resembling the prophets of old. Thou didst exhort, reprove, prophesy, and strengthen thy people, as well as the people of Europe and America.

Blessed are the peacemakers; and thou, O son of great peace, didst bring the true peace of Christ to thine own suffering people as well as to the whole Church and to the nations; wherefore we cry to thee, rejoice Christ's peacemaker for our troubled times.

Blessed are those whom men shall reproach and persecute and speak evil of for Christ's sake; and thou beloved Father Nikolai didst endure slander, imprisonment and exile, stirring up the fear and jealousy of the enemy against thee, and in all things thou didst prove to be the victor in Christ.

Glory, from St. Justin Popović, Tone 6

O holy Father Nikolai, the magnificence of thy glory shines forth for all to see, as thy divine brilliance illumines us all with the superabundant love of Christ the Prince of peace and humble Shepherd. Pray to Christ the only Lover of mankind, O most loving arch-shepherd, for us weak and decrepit sinners, that His mind, His brilliance, His care, His energy, His divinity, His strength, His sacrifice, His humility and His resurrected glory may shine within our hearts so that we may in some small way spread His love to the ends of the earth.

Both now: Theotokion in the same Tone

As the ladder to heaven, O Lady, Thou wast the means by which Christ came down and now, lift up thy children who in lowliness seek to climb the heavenly stair and protect us from every fall and deception.

Great Doxology and Troparia. Litanies. Dismissal. First Hour.

THE DIVINE LITURGY

On the Beatitudes, 8 troparia: 4 from Ode III of the canon of the Saint and 4 from Ode VI.

Prokimenon, in Tone 1: My mouth shall speak of wisdom, *and the meditation of my heart shall be of understanding.*
Verse: Hear this, all ye nations: give ear, all ye that inhabit the world.

THE READING FROM THE EPISTLE OF THE HOLY APOSTLE PAUL TO THE HEBREWS, § 318
(Heb. 7:26–8:2)

BRETHREN, for such a high priest became us, Who is holy, harmless, undefiled, separate from sinners, and made higher than the heavens; Who needeth not daily, as those high priests, to offer up sacrifice, first for his own sins, and then for the people's: for this He did once, when He offered up Himself. For the law maketh men high priests which have infirmity; but the word of the oath, which was since the law, maketh the Son, Who is consecrated for evermore. Now of the things which we have spoken this is the sum: We have such a high priest, Who is set on the right hand of the throne of the Majesty in the heavens; a minister of the sanctuary, and of the true tabernacle, which the Lord pitched, and not man.

41

Alleluia, in Tone 2: The mouth of the righteous shall meditate wisdom and his tongue shall speak judgment.

Verse: The law of God is in his heart, and in his steps shall he not be tripped.

The Reading from the Holy Gospel according to St. John, § 36 (John 10:9–16)

THE LORD SAID to the Jews who came to Him: "I am the door: by Me if any man enter in, he shall be saved, and shall go in and out, and find pasture. The thief cometh not, but for to steal, and to kill, and to destroy: I am come that they might have life, and that they might have it more abundantly. I am the good Shepherd: the good shepherd giveth his life for the sheep. But he that is a hireling, and not the shepherd, whose own the sheep are not, seeth the wolf coming, and leaveth the sheep, and fleeth; and the wolf catcheth them, and scattereth the sheep. The hireling fleeth, because he is a hireling, and careth not for the sheep. I am the good Shepherd, and know My sheep, and am known of Mine. As the Father knoweth Me, even so know I the Father: and I lay down My life for the sheep. And other sheep I have, which are not of this fold: them also I must bring, and they shall hear My voice; and there shall be one fold, and one shepherd."

Communion verse: In everlasting remembrance shall the righteous be; he shall not be afraid of evil tidings.

PRAYER
To our Holy and God-bearing Father
Hierarch Nikolai Velimirović
Bishop of Ohrid and Žiča
By St. Justin Popović

HOLY FATHER NIKOLAI, the magnificence of thy glory shines forth for all to see, as thy divine brilliance illumines us all with the superabundant love of Christ the Prince of peace and humble Shepherd. Pray to Christ the only Lover of mankind, O most loving arch-shepherd, for us weak and decrepit sinners, that His mind, His brilliance, His care, His energy, His divinity, His strength, His sacrifice, His humility and His resurrected glory may shine within our hearts so that we may in some small way spread His love to the ends of the earth. For to Him belong glory, honor, and worship, together with His unoriginate Father and life-giving Spirit, now and ever and unto the ages of ages. Amen.

ĪC·ХС НІ·КА

A Guide to Serbian Pronunciation

A a	"a" as in father		M m	"m" as in mother
B b	"b" as in boy		N n	"n" as in never
C c	"ts" as in tsar		Nj nj	"ñ" or "ny" as in canyon
Č č	"ch" as in chalk		O o	"o" as in gone or note
Ć ć	"ch" as in church		P p	"p" as in poem, not aspirated
D d	"d" as in door		R r	"r" heavily trilled
Dž dž	"j" as in edge		R r	as a vowel, "r" as in er
Đ đ	"j" as in jack		S s	"s" as in say
E e	"e" as in get		Š š	"sh" as in sugar
F f	"f" as in four		T t	"t" dental, not aspirated
G g	"g" as in go		U u	"oo" as in boot
H h	"kh," a guttural "h"		V v	"v" as in victory
I i	"i" as in pin or machine		Z z	"z" as in zoo
J j	"y" as in yes		Ž ž	"zh" as in azure & pleasure
K k	"k" as in kite, not aspirated		aj	"ay" as in cayak
L l	"l" as in leopard		ej	"ey" as in grey
Lj lj	"ly" as in million		oj	"oy" as in boy

www.ingramcontent.com/pod-product-compliance
Lightning Source LLC
Chambersburg PA
CBHW041545040426
42447CB00002B/50